A Note to Parents

DK READERS is a compelling program for beginning
readers, designed in conjunction with leading literacy
experts, including Dr. Linda Gambrell, Distinguished
Professor of Education at Clemson University.
Dr. Gambrell has served as President of the National
Reading Conference, the College Reading Association,
and the International Reading Association.

Beautiful illustrations and superb full-color photographs
combine with engaging, easy-to-read stories to offer a fresh
approach to each subject in the series. Each DK READER
is guaranteed to capture a child's interest while developing
his or her reading skills, general knowledge, and love
of reading.

The five levels of DK READERS are aimed at different
reading abilities, enabling you to choose the books that
are exactly right for your child:

Pre-level 1: Learning to read
Level 1: Beginning to read
Level 2: Beginning to read alone
Level 3: Reading alone
Level 4: Proficient readers

The "normal" age at which a child begins to read
can be anywhere from three to eight years old.
Adult participation through
the lower levels is very helpful
for providing encouragement,
discussing storylines, and
sounding out unfamiliar words.

No matter which level you
select, you can be sure that you
are helping your child learn to
read, then read to learn!

LONDON, NEW YORK, MUNICH,
MELBOURNE, AND DELHI

Editor Shari Last
Designer Rhys Thomas
Pre-Production Producer Marc Staples
Producer Louise Minihane
Managing Editor Elizabeth Dowsett
Design Manager Ron Stobbart
Publishing Manager Julie Ferris
Art Director Lisa Lanzarini
Publishing Director Simon Beecroft

Designed for DK by
Sandra Perry

Reading Consultant
Linda B. Gambrell, Ph.D.

First American Edition, 2014
14 15 16 17 10 9 8 7 6 5 4 3 2 1
Published in the United States by DK Publishing
4th Floor, 345 Hudson Street, New York, New York 10014

001–268987–Sep/14

Published in Great Britain by Dorling Kindersley Limited

DK books are available at special discounts when purchased in
bulk for sales promotions, premiums, fund-raising, or educational
use. For details, contact: DK Publishing Special Markets,
4th Floor, 345 Hudson Street, New York, New York 10014
SpecialSales@dk.com

A catalog record for this book is available
from the Library of Congress.

ISBN: 978-1-4654-2453-2 (Paperback)
ISBN: 978-1-4654-2452-5 (Hardcover)

Color reproduction by Alta Image, UK
Printed and bound in China by South China

Discover more at
www.dk.com
www.LEGO.com

Contents

DK READERS

LEGO MIXELS™

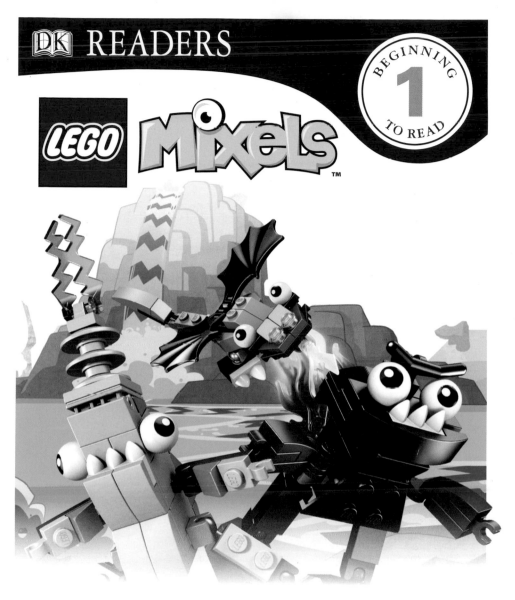

Meet the MIXELS™

Written by Shari Last

The Mixels™

What are these strange creatures?
They are Mixels!

Mixels are colorful, funny,
and always ready for adventure.

Let's meet the Mixels
and join in the fun.

Flain

Flain is a flaming Infernite.
He is so smart that his brain
sometimes bursts into flames!

The Infernites live in
a place full of hot lava
and rivers of fire.

Who else lives here?

lava

Vulk and Zorch

Vulk has red-hot hands, so
watch out for his high fives!

Zorch is a playful, fiery Infernite.
He speeds along,
leaving fire
trailing
behind him.

fiery

Krader, Seismo, and Shuff

The hardworking Cragsters spend their time digging underground tunnels. Krader has a wrecking ball fist.

wrecking ball

Seismo's huge feet can smash rocks.

Shuff is strong, but also a little clumsy. Oops!

Teslo, Zaptor, and Volectro

Who are these crazy Mixels?

They are Teslo, Zaptor, and Volectro.

These yellow Electroids
are full of sizzling energy.
They live high in the mountains,
where they catch lightning.

Flurr, Lunk, and Slumbo

Brrr. It is cold here.

Let's meet the Frosticons

who live in frozen volcanoes.

This is Flurr.

This is Lunk.

Can you spot Slumbo?

Slumbo is very, very relaxed.

He is nearly always asleep.

Scorpi, Footi, and Hoogi

Hello, Spikels!

Scorpi loves pillow fights,
but beware his prickly tail!

Footi cannot
sit still.
His spiky feet
are always
moving.

Hoogi always
wants to cuddle,
but his claws
sometimes get
in the way.

Jawg, Gobba, and Chomly

The Fang Gang are always hungry. Jawg has huge teeth for fast chewing.

Gobba's tongue can find the best food around.

Chomly will eat... ANYTHING!
His bad breath keeps everyone
else away.

Kraw, Tentro, and Balk

Welcome to the crazy, stretchy Rubberlands.
The funny Flexers live here.

Kraw loves bouncing up and down.

Tentro climbs everything with his powerful tentacles.

tentacles

Balk's hammerhead makes him easy to spot!

Glomp, Glurt, and Torts

The gooey Glorp Corp live in the wet, muddy swamps.

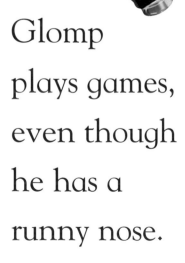

Glomp plays games, even though he has a runny nose.

Glurt
dribbles when
he is happy.

Torts is messy.
His slimy hands make
everything sticky.

Magnifo, Mesmo, and Wizwuz

Introducing the Wiztastics!
These magicians love
to put on a show.

Magnifo wants
his magic to
be amazing.

magician

Mesmo is his shy assistant.

Wizwuz loves performing,
even if he sometimes
makes mistakes.

Let's Party!

Now that you have met the Mixels, it is time to play. Bring some food, a pot of goo, a magic wand, a cozy pillow, and a fire extinguisher.

Let's have some fun!

Mix Festival

Quiz

1. Which Mixels live in a place full of hot lava?

2. Which Cragster has a wrecking ball fist?

3. Which Mixels are yellow?

4. Which Mixel is nearly always asleep?

5. Who loves pillow fights?

6. Who has bad breath?

7. Where do
the Flexers live?

8. What does Kraw love doing?

9. Whose hands
make everything
sticky?

10. What color
are the Wiztastics?

Answers on page 31

Glossary

lava
hot, melted rock that
flows above ground

fiery
something made
of fire or flames

wrecking ball
a big, heavy ball that
knocks things down

tentacles
a flexible part of the
body used to touch
or climb things

magician
a person who
performs magic

Index

Answers to the quiz on pages 28 and 29:
1. The Infernites 2. Krader 3. The Electroids
4. Slumbo 5. Scorpi 6. Chomly
7. The Rubberlands 8. Bouncing 9. Torts 10. Purple

Here are some other DK Readers you might enjoy.

Level 1

Star Wars®: Are Ewoks Scared of Stormtroopers?
Meet the bravest heroes in the _Star Wars_ galaxy,
who defeat evil villains against all odds.

The LEGO® Movie: Calling All Master Builders!
Who are the Master Builders? Do they have
what it takes to stop Lord Business's evil plans?

LEGO® _Star Wars_®: A New Hope
The evil Empire has built a dangerous weapon!
Can the rebels save the galaxy?

Level 2

The LEGO® Movie: Awesome Adventures
Meet Emmet and join him on his extraordinary
quest to save the universe!

Star Wars®: The Adventures of C-3PO
Meet C-3PO, a clever protocol droid. Join him
on his exciting adventures across the galaxy.

LEGO® Friends: Perfect Pets
Learn all about Mia, Olivia, Andrea, Stephanie, and Emma's
pets—and discover how much fun pets can be!